To Feel the Night in Other Places

-poetry by Ashton Rhodes

☆

I travel to feel

The night

in other places.

☆

I want to drive until

the stars speak

another language.

My car is a time machine
depending on the song
that's playing.

☆

Beats from the stereo
match hearts in meditation.
Close your eyes, be anywhere.

Convertible top open
we drive through the desert like
bandits who've stolen the stars.

☆

From your passenger's seat
I watch power lines
dissect the night sky.

<u>No Greater Immortality</u>

*Somewhere between the reckless
abandon of youth and the wisdom
and experience of age, exists the
centrifugal force of life, spinning us
away from the center we crave.*

*The illusion of wholeness and the
fault of man; To see time as linear and
strive to stay on its path.*

☆

I've saved moments like coins

earning interest in my mind.

It's time to sell the story.

☆

Letters neatly arranged

into lines;

No greater immortality.

The plight of the creative mind;
We build worlds for others
but sit alone with our blueprints.

☆

We travel the infinite highways
of our mind, some read maps,
I prefer to throw darts.

*To be trapped in the conformity
of responsibility is poison to the
artist who thrives on uncertainty.*

☆

*You can never know in whose
story you'll land a starring role.*

I want the marrow of life
the very core, the part that
could kill me if swallowed.

☆

On the nights I lose
my sleep, I gain moments
I'll come to dream of.

In past tense there are only
memories. Write your life
in the present.

☆

We are all children chasing days
into the future, but most
forget to have fun while running.

Man's creativity lies bleeding
in this society of flaccid passion.
Erect your imagination.

☆

The real adventure begins
when you stop
making plans.

Change opens the door

to your next great adventure.

☆

Our Worship Lights the Stars

His cloak is made of ferns and moss.

_His hair is long and wild like the
winds that stir the leaves to dance._

_His mouth speaks words of the wood,
a long forgotten magic tongue that
calls the trees to sway._

_I wish to be a faun in his castle so
that I might run along beside him as
he paints the forest green._

☆

We are light delighting in flesh,
forever seeking the
mirror to guide us home.

☆

I've drawn spirals all my life
outward to in, ever seeking
the center of my labyrinth.

The naked trees are maps
made of arteries and veins
leading ever upward and below.

☆

That night in the forest,
the stars swore secrecy as
we made love to the earth.

Half naked branches of early fall

open windows to starry secrets

hidden by summer's warmth.

☆

I am the moon maiden.

Orion comes to me in dreams.

Our worship lights the stars.

The leaves are dancing with

the wind, spinning paths

that lead to magic.

☆

How do the trees not tire

of their rooted feet?

I always long to run.

I am your moon.

You are my gravity.

Together we make waves.

☆

If I fall any farther,

I'll be falling up.

Your voice shifts my polarity.

Dark blue night.

Shooting star, you look at me,

"No need."

☆

You remind me of a fairytale.

I dance in your forest

for you spared my savage heart.

In your atmosphere I burn.
Your alchemy transforms me
from a falling star, into gold.

☆

I seek the shadows in you
and whisper midnight verses
to make your sun rise.

I hide my heart in words.

You read between the lines.

☆

I hunt the man who
feeds the wolf
within my soul.

Ice covered branches bear the
weight of spring's promise,
heavy as a lover's goodbye.

☆

In the purple hour between
dark and dawn, magic reigns
while stars kiss the sun.

In a faraway world, we place our magic things and fairy rings.

We bind them to our make believe and seldom seen.

Those fragile days of summers past, child's feet in summer grass,

bright moon shone on midnight's trees, mud was brushed from dirty knees.

We knew the way when we were young, and from our fingers web was spun,

to swing from stars and race the dew, to laugh and tumble with the few

who still believed in magic things and never left their fairy rings.

☆

Arsons

My skin the kindle, your fingertips
the flame.

The heat between our blood,

burns me,

unfolds me

like a seed that only blooms through
fire.

And we emerge

drenched in the ash of

total consumption.

☆

I Know Your Lyrics by Heart

I want to be filled moment to moment by ecstasy.

I want to live like the wind.

I want to move in the mystery and dance for you within the flames.

I want to be embraced by the earth until I dissolve like dew at the sun's touch and quietly evaporate, until dusk when I come to life again in the moonlight.

☆

I am a secret you cannot
share. I know the shape of
your lips in the stolen darkness.

☆

He whispers to me,
"Lie back, don't' be afraid,
we're all cannibals in bed."

I bleed too freely
to play with your
razor-sharp charms.

☆

The atmosphere is heavy with
lust and soft evening rain. Jazz
plays from a street corner sax.

Slow crooning from a record
player, velvet notes as smooth as
the wine between our lips.

☆

Neon shivers above the door.
Smoke filled crooner bar
edge of Chicago, meet me there.

Upright bass snaps, piano trills,
bartender pours scotch. This place
is all blue velvet and brass.

☆

Paris in the rain. Three streets to
the hotel. I can't wait,
take me here...now.

You smell of bourbon and rebellion. I want to kiss you until even my skin is intoxicated.

☆

The light caressed her body like a voyeur witnessing something secret.

Cobbled streets reflect neon
in the rain. Why rush home?
This is the magic hour.

☆

I follow shadows across your
skin. My lips trace the edge of
light as I devour your darkness.

I want to hold you

until there is nothing

left of me.

☆

And suddenly you stood

before me, a dream made flesh

by racing hearts and hungry eyes.

As clouds rolled in, the wind told me your name, but I did not hear it.

When the rain soaked my skin, I felt you in my blood, but I did not know it.

The moonlight gave me visions of your eyes, but I did not see them.

But when your voice pierced the veil surrounding me, I was filled with your presence.

Suddenly I knew everything that the rain and the wind had shown me.

I recalled a hundred times your name whispered in my ear, a hundred times your eyes before me in my dreams.

And in my blood, the fire I felt was the knowledge of stars and the light we both carry, one light, the light of our souls that searched the earth hundreds of times for the other.

And a hundred times I would die just to have the joy of finding you again and again.

☆

A Sense of Time and Stillness

I see my soul as a string that unravels
and ends up somewhere across the
globe,

or the street, maybe even across time.

With hopes that one day someone
will find it lying at their feet and say,

"So this is where I left you?"

And I'll feel the pull from a million
miles away or from the other room,
and suddenly from that tug, I'll have
a sense of time and stillness, of
tension and weight, and the
knowledge of balance.

☆

I have fallen perpetually
a star out of place, searching
for the night inside you.

☆

My shore I procure for your
arrival. I have combed the
sands awaiting your tide.

You are the music
my soul has danced to.
I know your lyrics by heart.

☆

You make my heart race
with only your words. Imagine
what your hands could do.

Your poetry breaks the skin,

tattooing me with verses

I'll wear like a new dress.

☆

Blanket on the hood of your

Bel Air. Stars above, earth below

and heaven in your eyes.

He was the Earth
and I was the moon that crested
all of his domain in beauty.

☆

In an ocean of stars, across
ageless waters, your eyes have
been my northern star.

I am a narcissist.
I see my soul reflected in yours
and I can't stop staring.

☆

I want a second star to
the right and straight on 'til
morning, kind of love.

<u>Forever is Not Enough</u>

*This long journey to your arms, this
waiting in loneliness for the touch
that awakens remnants of a life
before.*

*The kiss that ignites the dream of a
thousand lives together. Reunited as
one in this embrace. Millions of years
could not destroy this love, born time
and again from darkness. Our love
unending, unyielding to time.*

*Forever is not enough for us.
This love is the multiplying universe,
it is the creation and the divine. It is
every fiber of life, every breath of
every living thing born from the same
spark of love, replicating itself in our
single kiss.*

☆